SAMSUNG GA
CAMERA USE

A Beginners Manual to Master All
Camera Features of Samsung Galaxy S22,
S22 Plus, and S22 Ultra, and Take
Professional Photos and Videos:
Including Camera Tips

By

Nath Jones

Table of content

INTRODUCTION

The new Samsung Galaxy S22 series has been the rave since its released. A lot has been said and written about this power smartphone: its new processor, gorgeous design, and truckload of features and functionalities. What has had little coverage though is the cameras.

I mean, it's no secret that the Samsung flagship devices come with some of the most powerful cameras in the smartphone industry. But just how much more powerful the Galaxy S22 series, particularly S22 Ultra's camera is, has not been explored fully.

This user manual seeks to fix that. The content herein focuses on the Samsung Galaxy S22 series cameras; with special interest placed on the S22 Ultra.

This is not to say that you will be left out if you have any of the other devices in the series (S22 and S22 Plus). On the contrary, this book contains sufficient information required to enable all S22 series users master the use of all the cameras on their device.

There is a high chance that you are under-using the cameras in your smartphone. Not to worry though, by the time you are done studying this user guide, you will be able to perform all possible functions with your device cameras, and take breathtaking pictures.

This manual carefully explores all features and offers an understandable guide for you to navigate through your Samsung S22's Camera seamlessly.

Let's get right to it!

CHAPTER ONE

Rear Camera Capacity

The rear camera setup includes:

- 12MP Ultra-Wide Camera
- Pixel size: 1.4μm
- FOV: 120°
- F.No (aperture): F2.2
- 1/2.55" image sensor size
- 2x50MP Wide-angle Camera
- Dual Pixel AF, OIS
- Pixel size: 1.0μm (12MP 2.0μm)
- FOV: 85°
- F.No (aperture): F1.8
- 1/1.56" image sensor size
- 3x10MP Telephoto Camera
- Pixel size: 1.0μm
- FOV: 36°
- F.No (aperture): F2.4
- 1/3.94" image sensor size

Space Zoom

3x Optical Zoom

Super Resolution Zoom up to 30x

Selfie camera capacity

- 1x10MP Selfie Camera
- Dual Pixel AF
- Pixel size: 1.22μm
- FOV: 80°
- F.No (aperture): F2.2
- 1/3.24" image sensor size

CHAPTER TWO

How to use Galaxy S22 camera quick launch

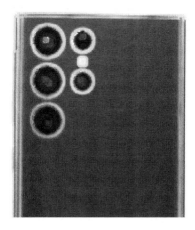

When you complete your purchase, you can unbox your brand-new Galaxy S22. This will reveal your sleek device. The device's side key will open the camera app almost immediately when you press it twice. That's how to activate the camera quick launch on your Galaxy S22. Other Samsung Galaxy devices using One UI as well as most Android devices have this feature.

You'll find the side key on the right side of your device. Press it twice for the camera quick launch even without unlocking your device.

When you perform the camera quick launch without unlocking your device, it will only be possible to view photos that you take during the current session. Other photos on the devices will not be accessible until you unlock your device. This also happens when you click on the camera icon from the lock screen. This is only a security measure.

How to Enable or Disable Galaxy S22 Camera Quick Launch

On the Galaxy S22, the camera quick launch feature is switched on by default. When the camera doesn't launch after performing the quick launch steps, it means that the feature is turned off.

Launch Settings from the device's Application screen or Home screen. You can also launch settings from the quick settings panel by clicking on the Settings icon.

Proceed to click on Advanced features. From here, you can personalize different features on your device. Select the camera quick launch and touch the side key.

You can customize the Side Key function with two gestures. Double press and long press.

The Side key's double press gesture is set to activate or deactivate the camera quick launch.

CHAPTER THREE

Taking A Picture

To take a picture, open the Camera application from the App drawer or Home Screen.

It is important to note that:

❖ When you perform the camera quick launch without unlocking your device, it will only be possible to view photos that you take during the current session. Other photos on the devices will not be accessible until you unlock your device. This also happens when you click on the camera icon from the lock screen. This is only a security measure

❖ The camera application will shut off automatically when it is not in use.

❖ Depending on your device model or service provider, some features won't be available.

Click on the subject in the preview screen to set the camera focus.

❖ Tap and move the adjustment bar which appears below or below the circular frame in either direction. This will adjust the picture's brightness.

❖ Click on the circular frame to take a photo.

❖ Change the shooting mode by dragging the shooting modes list rightward or leftward. Alternatively, you can swipe rightward or leftward on the preview screen to toggle the shooting mode.

Click on the white shutter icon at the middle bottom part of the screen to take a photo.

- ❖ Depending on which shooting mode is set and camera in use, the preview screen will have different outlays.
- ❖ When the subject is too close to the camera, the focus may not be clearly visible. It is ideal to take the videos or photos from a good distance.

❖ Try cleaning camera lens if the pictures or videos appear blurry when shooting.

❖ Ensure that the device's lens is not contaminated or damaged, if not, the device won't function properly with high resolution modes.

❖ The Galaxy S22's camera has a wide-angle lens feature. With this, it is not abnormal to find minor distortion occurring in wide-angle videos or pictures. This does not necessarily translate into a dysfunctional device.

❖ The resolution in use will determine the maximum capacity for video recording.

❖ When there is a sudden change in the air temperature, it is possible for the camera to form condensation. This is because of the different temperatures inside the camera cover and outside it. You can try to avoid this when you want to use the camera application. Let the camera dry naturally before shooting videos or taking pictures to avoid blurriness from fogging.

How to Take Selfies

It is possible to take selfie portraits using the device's front camera.

1) Click on the rotate icon at the bottom right corner to toggle between the front and rear camera.

2) Hold up the camera to your face and stare into the front camera lens. Click

on the wide-angle icon to take wide-angle shots of people or the landscape.

3) Click on the camera icon to take a photo.

Applying Filter and Beauty Effects

It is possible to modify the features of your face like your face shape, and skin tone before you take a picture. You can also choose a filter effect.

1) Touch the wand icon at the top right corner on the preview screen.

2) Proceed to choose effects and then take a photo.

With the My Filters feature, it is possible to generate your unique filter with an image's color tone you like from your device's gallery.

The device's camera automatically suggests what composition would be ideal for your picture by recognizing the angle and position of the subject.

1) Touch the settings icon on the preview screen and then proceed to toggle the Shot Suggestions either on or off.

2) Select Photo on the shooting modes list.

    A pop-up guide should be visible from the preview screen.

3) Position the guide at the subject. The device's camera will then recognize

the image's composition and recommend a composition on the preview screen.

4) Try moving the device around to help the guide match the composition recommended. The guide will switch to a yellow color when the ideal composition is being achieved.

Touch the camera icon to take a photo.

How to Use the Camera Button

Touch and hold down the white shutter icon in order to record a video.

You can take burst shots by swiping the camera button to the screen's edge and then holding it.

It is possible to take pictures conveniently when you can click the shutter icon from anywhere on the device's screen. To activate this feature, click on Shooting Modes and toggle the Floating Shutter button switch either on or off.

How to Use Zoom in Features

You can choose .6/1/3/10, move it to the right or left to zoom out or in. Also, you can pinch two of your fingers on the screen to zoom out, and spread out both fingers to zoom in. A zoom guide will be visible on your device's screen to show what part of the image you are zooming in on. This only happens when the zoom ratio has exceeded a particular level.

1. 6: The Ultra-wide camera will allow you to record wide angle videos and take wide angle pictures of various subjects such as landscapes.

2. 1: The wide-angle camera makes it possible for normal and basic pictures or videos to be taken or recorded.

3. 3: You can enlarge the subject when taking pictures or recording videos with the telephoto camera (3x).

4. 10: You can enlarge the subject when taking pictures or recording videos with the telephoto camera (10x).

CHAPTER FOUR

Portrait Mode / Portrait Video Mode

With the Samsung S22 camera, you can capture videos or pictures with a blurred background and the subject standing out very visibly. It is possible to add a background effect which you can edit after snapping a picture.

1) Click on Portrait or Portrait Video under More in the Shooting Modes list.

2) Touch background effect and choose the background effect you'd prefer. Move the adjustment bar's slider when you want to adjust the background effect's intensity.

3) Click on the shutter icon or the record button to snap a picture or record a video respectively whenever you're ready.

❖ Depending on the mode of shooting, some options may or may not be available.

❖ This feature is ideal in an environment with adequate light.

❖ In certain conditions which will be listed below, the background blur feature may not function optimally. They include:

  ➢ When the subject or device is in motion.

  ➢ When the subject is transparent or thin.

  ➢ When the background has a similar color to the subject.

> When the background or subject is plain.

Pro Mode / Pro Video Mode

You can record videos or take pictures and tweak different shooting options like ISO and exposure values simultaneously.

Click on More and then select Pro or Pro Video on the shooting modes.

Choose options and then proceed to personalize the settings.

Then you can click on the shutter icon or the record button to snap a picture or record a video respectively whenever you're ready.

Available options

1) **Settings Reset**

2) **ISO**: Choose an ISO value. This feature controls the camera light sensitivity. High values are used for dimly-lit or fast-moving objects while low values are used for brightly-lit or static objects. However, it is important to note that using high values for ISO settings could result in noisy photos or videos.

3) **SPEED**: Control the speed of the shutter. With a slow shutter speed, greater amounts of light is allowed in, thereby making the videos or picture brighter. This setting is best for taking videos or pictures taken at night or of scenery. Conversely, a quick shutter speed permits lesser amounts of lights while recording videos or taking pictures. This setting

is best for taking pictures or recording videos of fast-moving subjects.

4) **EV:** Switch or toggle the exposure value. The exposure value controls the amount of light received by the camera's sensor. When there's not much light, it is ideal to use an exposure value that is high.

5) **FOCUS**: Adjust the focus mode. Move the adjustment bar's slider when you want to adjust the focus.

6) **WB**: Choose an adequate white balance so that recorded images or pictures possess a true-to-life color range. It is possible to adjust the color temperature.

7) **MIC**: Choose the direction you would want to record its sound at a higher

level. It's also possible to use a Bluetooth Microphone or USB by connecting it to your device.

8) **ZOOM**: Set the zoom speed (Pro video mode).

Recording High-Resolution Pro Videos

Record high-resolution pro videos with a maximum resolution of 8K.

1. Click on FHD (30) and then swipe the top panel to the right. You should find 8k (24) at the top left corner, click on it to record a pro video.

2. When you're done recording a pro video, you can play it using the Gallery application. When you click on a frame that you prefer, this frame will be saved as a high-resolution picture.

CHAPTER FIVE

Separating the Focus Area and the Exposure Area

Using the steps below, it is possible to separate the focus/ exposure area.

1) Click and hold down the preview screen.

2) Automatically, the AF/AE frame would be displayed on the screen. Move the frame towards the area which you want to separate the focus area and the exposure area.

How to Activate Tracking Autofocus

Auto focus makes it possible to quickly lock in on a chosen point or area in a bid to prejudice sharper images

- Launch the Camera app.

- Open Photos by swiping

- Tap your finger on an area on the screen and then click on the auto focus icon to switch on Auto Focus.

- Touch the capture button to take a picture when you're ready.

- Captured picture will be available for viewing in the Gallery Application.

How to Activate Night Mode

In dimly-lit conditions, you can take pictures without using the camera's flash light. With a tripod, you will get even steadier and brighter pictures.

1) Click on More and then select Night on the shooting modes. You may have clearer photos when you set the time

that is displayed on the screen's right bottom.

2) Click on the shutter button and steadily position your device until you are done shooting.

CHAPTER SIX

Food Mode

Use vibrant colors when taking pictures of your meals.

1) Click on More and then proceed to select **Food** on the shooting modes list.

2) Touch the screen and then move the circular frame to the area you want to highlight. When you do this, the area that is outside the circular frame will become blurred. You can resize the circular frame by dragging a corner of the frame.

3) Click and move the adjustment bar to set the color tone.

4) Proceed to click on the shutter icon to take a picture.

Shoot scenes like moving cars and people and then view them as quick-motion videos.

1) Click on More and then proceed to select Hyper-lapse on the shooting modes list.

2) Touch the frame rate icon to choose a frame rate option. The Galaxy S22 will automatically set the frame rate to match the changing rate of the scene if you select it.

3) Touch the record icon to being recording.

4) Touch the stop button to complete recording.

How to Use the Bokeh Effect While Taking Pictures

1) Launch the Camera application

2) Proceed to select the Live Focus mode.

3) Set the blue intensity to your preference with the adjustment bar displayed on your screen.

4) Take the picture immediately you achieve the blur effect that you want.

CHAPTER SEVEN

How to Use the Face Effects

You can use the face effects feature to eliminate red eye, make your eyes appear bigger and even brighten the tone of your skin.

1) Launch the Gallery application and then choose the picture that you want to edit.

2) Touch the Edit icon and the click on the three dots for more options. When you do that, proceed to click on Face Effects.

3) It is possible to choose from a wealth of editing alternatives. These options include red eye fix, tone and smoothness.

4) When you tap on an option, adhere to the recommendations that would

appear on your screen. Alternatively, you can move the slider to set your preferred intensity. In example, spot fixer will help you to eliminate face blemishes when you click on certain areas of the person's face. You can use the arrows to redo or undo your edits

5) Click on Done when you have finished editing.

6) Should you need to start over, you can click on Revert and then click on Revert to Original.

7) Click on Save and then touch Save again to save your newly-edited photo to your device. Maintain the original picture on your device by clicking on the three vertical dots to open More options. Proceed to click

on Save as copy to keep the original
picture.

Panorama Mode

With the Panorama mode, you can take
multiple pictures and then join them
together to create a picture with wide
scene.

1) To use this feature, open More and
   then select Panorama on the
   Shooting modes list.

2) Touch the shutter button and then
   slowly move the phone in one
   direction.

   Maintain the image inside the frame
   on the camera's viewfinder. When the
   preview image is not inside the guide
   frame, or stop moving the device, the

camera will stop taking the pictures automatically.

3) Touch the Stop icon to stop taking pictures.

   Try to not take pictures of indistinct backgrounds like a plain wall or an empty sky.

Single Take Mode

Snap different pictures and videos with just one shot.

The Galaxy S22 will select the best shot automatically and create pictures with videos or filters with certain sections repeated.

1) Click on More and then select Single Take on the shooting modes list.

This should open up the Single Take Mode.

Click on the icon at the top right corner to choose what kind of images to capture in the single take mode. Click on an option to select or deselect it.

2) Touch the shutter icon when you want to capture a particular scene. This should begin a timer.

3) Touch the preview thumbnail to see the result when you are done.

You can see other results by dragging the widget upwards. Individually save the results by clicking on Select and then ticking the items you would like to save. Then proceed to click on the arrow facing down.

CHAPTER EIGHT

Super Slow-Mo Mode

The Super slow-mo is one feature that helps you to efficiently record a quickly-passing moment slowly in a way you can appreciate later.

1) Click on More and select Super Slow-Mo in the shooting modes list and then click on the record icon to record a video. The device will record the moment in a really slow motion and then save it on your device as a video.

2) Click on the preview thumbnail on the preview screen to see your video.

3) Touch the pencil icon and move the section editing bar to the right or left

in order to edit the super slow-mo video.

It is ideal to use this feature in an environment with sufficient lighting. If you record a video indoors with poor lighting or insufficient light, the device's screen may appear grainy or dark. The device's screen can flicker in certain lighting conditions like environments with fluorescent lighting.

Recording Super Slow-Motion Videos Automatically

You can record videos in a really slow motion automatically. This will record videos once motion detected in the motion detection area. Touch the icon to activate it. The motion detection feature will be turned on and the motion detection area will be displayed on the preview screen.

1) Touch the record icon to begin recording. When motion has been detected, the camera will begin recording in a really slow motion. Your video will also be saved onto your device automatically.

Super Slow-mo recording may begin at a wrong time when any of the following conditions are is present:

The device shakes or another object moves near the subject that is in the motion detection area.

Recording in certain lighting conditions like environments with fluorescent lighting.

Slow Motion Mode

Capture a moment to view it in slow motion. It's possible to appropriate the parts of your video you want to be played I slow motion.

1) Click on More in the shooting modes list and then select Slow Motion. Next click on the record icon to start recording a video.

2) Click on the square stop icon to stop recording.

3) Touch the preview thumbnail on the preview screen to view your video.

The video's quick segment will be turned into a slow-motion section, and the video will begin to play. Based on the footage, up to two slow motion portions will be made.

You can edit the slow-motion section by clicking on the pencil icon and then dragging the section editing bar to the right or left.

CHAPTER NINE

Video Mode

Automatically, the camera will adjust the shooting options depending on the environment. This is to record videos easily.

1) Click on Video on the shooting modes list and the touch the record icon to begin recording a video.

   a) You can switch between the rear and front camera while you are recording by swiping down or upwards. Alternatively, you can touch the rotate icon to switch cameras.

   b) You can also take a picture from the video while you are still recording. Touch the Camera shutter icon to do this.

c) You record a sound from a particular direction more by pointing the camera in that direction and then adjusting the zoom.

2) Touch the Stop icon to finish recording your video.

a) The video quality may deteriorate in order to stop the device from overheating when you use the video zoom feature for a long time.

b) In dimly-lit environments, the optical zoom feature may not work.

How to Add Background Music to Video

1) Open the video that you would like to edit. It is possible to find any video by

either opening the Gallery or launching the Camera application on your device.

2) Click on the edit option. Typically, this option is found below the video when you open it from the preview mode in the Gallery application.

3) Proceed to click on Movie Maker. This should take automatically to the Samsung Galaxy Store App. Here, you can easily download and install the Samsung Movie Maker app.

4) Touch install and proceed to download and install the movie maker on to your device.

5) Launch the Movie Maker. With the Movie Maker now installed, you can now access more video editing features by launching it.

6) Click on the plus sign (+) icon. You will find this gray button at the bottom-right corner of your device's screen. Clicking on it will pick a new video for editing. Depending on the video editing app you may be using, this option may differ.

7) Choose the video you would want to edit. After opening the menu for choosing a new video, click on the icon for the folder that contains your saved video and then select Done to upload it to Movie Maker.

8) In the Template menu, click on Custom. It will then be possible to add a template to your video when you upload it. Select Done to open the basic video editor menu.

9) Click on the white plus (+) icon that appears on the bottom-left of the video editor. This will allow you to add new elements to your video.

10) Click on the Audio Tab. This will bring up the menu that will allow you to add audio to your video include. This includes any music that you may have saved on your device.

11) Choose your preferred music for your video. With the menu for adding audio open, you can navigate and select any music file on your device to add to your video.

12) Set the audio volume. Scroll downwards in the editing menu on the screen's right side to reveal the Volume option. This is represented

by a speaker icon. Touch it to bring up the master volume controls.

13) Proceed to save your video. With the music you added synced to with your video, you can now press Save on the screen's left side in the main video editing menu. Choose where you prefer to save it to and watch it later.

How to Combine Multiple Video Clips into One

- Launch the Gallery app.

- Navigate to the video you would like to include in your project.

- Touch the edit button at the bottom left corner of the device's screen. It should look like a pencil.

- Click on Add at the screen's top and then select a second video to combine with the first video. It is possible to select still images and multiple clips and then click on Done when you are ready. Locate one of the videos you want to include in your project.

CHAPTER TEN

How to Add Effects During Video Call

This changes or edits the background when you are making a video call. This feature also blocks background noise during video calls.

Click on Advanced Features on the Settings screen and then select Video call effects.

Touch the switch to toggle it on or off. The icon will be visible when you are making a video call on the video calling apps screen.

Viewing Brighter and Clearer Videos

Improve your videos' image quality in order to enjoy more vivid and brighter colors.

Open Settings app and then click on Advanced features. Proceed to click on Video Brightness and then select Bright.

• This feature is only available in some apps.

• Using this feature may cause your device's battery to drain quickly.

How to View Videos

Open the Gallery all and choose a video you would like to play. You can swipe right or left on the screen to see other files.

Touch the three vertical dots at the bottom right corner of the screen and then select Open in Video Player to use more options during video playback.

Dragging your finger upwards or downwards on the left part of the playback screen will adjust the brightness. Dragging your finger upwards or downwards on the right part of the playback screen will adjust the volume.

You can fast-forward or rewind the video by sliding your finger horizontally on the screen either to the left or right side.

CHAPTER ELEVEN

Using Video Call Effects

Click on the video icon on the screen of the video calling app. Click on:

- **Reset all:** To reset the entire video call settings to default.

- **Background**: To blur or change the background during video calls.

- **Auto framing**: Deactivate or activate the auto framing feature. This feature enables the device to change the zoom and shooting angle automatically why tracking and recognizing people during a video call when it is activated.

- **Mic mode**: This ensures clearer sound by blocking background noise.

– **Standard**: Removes all noise so that it sounds just as a normal voice call.

– **Voice focus:** Focuses on the sound coming from the direction of the front camera.

– **All sound:** Transmits the entire sounds around you like the sound of other people, background music.

- **Settings**: Add or select images or background cookies to be in use during video calls.

It is important to note that:

Depending on the device model, most features won't be available.

Most features will only be available when the front camera is in use.

Take a screenshot when you are using the device. You can decide to draw or write on it. You can also decide to crop or share the screenshot. It is possible to capture the scrollable area and current screen.

Screenshots can be viewed in the Gallery application. To take a screenshot, follow the instructions below:

Hold the volume down key and the side key down simultaneously. This will take a screenshot. This is the Key Capture method.

Alternatively, you can use the swipe capture method. This would require you to swipe your hand across the screen either leftward or rightward.

There are some apps and features that would restrict you from taking a screenshot.

You may need to activate the swipe capture method, if the swipe capture method does not take a screenshot. To activate it, open Settings and click on Advanced features. Proceed to click on Motion and gestures and then select the Palm swipe to capture feature to activate it.

When you finish taking a screenshot, you can perform a number of functions with it using the toolbar at the screen's bottom. These functions include:

1) Capture an entire page (like a webpage), both the part visible on the screen and the part not visible. When

this is done, the screen will automatically swipe downwards to screenshot the rest of the page not in view.

2) Draw or write on a captured screenshot. You can also crop a part out of a captured screenshot. The cropped part will be available for viewing in you Gallery app.

3) Include tags to your captured screenshot. You can search for screenshots using the tags. Click on Search at the top area of the Apps Screen and then select Screenshots. It is possible to see the tags list and easily sort for the screenshot you are looking for.

4) Share your captured screenshot with others.

If these functions are not readily visible from the captured screen, open the Settings app and then touch Advanced Features. Click on Screenshots and Screen recorder and then select the Screenshot toolbar switch to switch it on.

CHAPTER TWELVE

How to Use the Screen Record

Make a recording of your screen while you are using your device.

1) Launch the notification panel, scroll downwards and then touch the screen recorder icon to activate it.

2) Choose a sound setting and then click on Start Recording. A countdown will begin, after which your recording will start.

   You can write or draw on the screen by selecting the pencil icon

   You can record your screen with a video overlay of yourself by clicking on the icon.

3) Click on the Stop icon when you are done with your recording.

Your screen record will be available for viewing in the Gallery app.

Change the screen recorder settings by opening the settings app and then clicking on Advanced Features. Select Screenshots and Screen recorder.

Capturing an Area from a Video

While a video is being played, you can choose a portion of the video and capture it as a GIF animation.

If you have a content that you would like to capture during a video playback, simply:

1) Open the Air command panel and then click on Smart Select.

2) Touch GIF on the toolbar

3) Set the size and position of the area you want to capture.

4) Click on Record to begin capturing.

   a) Before capturing a video, you should make sure that the video is playing.

   b) The maximum capturing duration will be shown on your device screen.

   c) If you are capturing an area from a video, the sound will not be recorded.

5) To stop capturing, click on Stop.

6) Choose an option to use with the chosen area.

   a) You can either draw or write on it. Click on the pencil icon to do this. Tap the play button to see the finished project before proceeding to save the file to your device.

b) Click on the share icon to share the area you have selected with others.

c) Use the arrow facing downwards to save your file onto your device.

Stabilizing Videos (Super Steady)

You can put this feature to use when there is a lot of shaking while you are recording a video.

Click on Video on the Shooting Modes List and then select the Shooting options to activate the video stabilization feature. After this, you can record a video.

Utilize the auto framing feature and adjust the device to change the zoom and shorting angle automatically by tracking and recognizing people while recording videos.

Click on Video in the Shooting modes list and the touch shaky hand icon to activate it. After this, you can record a video.

It is possible to track and adjust the shooting angle as well as zoom in on a particular individual. To do this, just click on the frame that is displayed around the person. You can deactivate the tracking feature by clicking on the frame again.

CHAPTER THIRTEEN

How to Turn on 8K Video Capture

Record videos in the highest possible resolution.

Launch the video mode from inside the Camera app.

Proceed to click on the aspect ratio icon and then you will see the 8K 24 option.

How to Use scene optimizer to improve your photos:

The scene optimizer makes use of artificial intelligence (AI) in improving your pictures. It also allows longer handheld night photos.

1) Open the Camera app and then click on the settings icon at the top left part of the screen.

2) Proceed to switch the Scene optimizer on

3) Snap a picture and then you will notice that it auto-adjusts using a dual circular icon to indicate that the camera has made optimization.

How to Extract High Resolution Image from a Video

You can take still images from video Galaxy 22.

1) Launch the Samsung Video player app or open the Gallery.

2) Navigate to the video which you would like to take a photo from.

3) Begin playing the video and then click on the Quick crop icon at the screen's bottom left corner.

Move the video's duration bar to the point where you would like you capture your image.

4) The preview image will be visible at the screen's bottom left corner.

5) You can open the Gallery app to find the picture you captured by searching the Video Captures folder.

CHAPTER FOURTEEN

Capturing an Area from a Video

Chose a portion of a video that you would like to capture as a GIF animation.

If you have a content that you would like to capture during a video playback, simply:

1) Open the Air command panel and then click on Smart Select.

2) Touch the capture icon on the toolbar

3) Set the size and position of the area you want to capture.

How to Edit the Available Camera Modes

Remove or add modes that are more essential.

1) Click on More and you will find and "Add +" visible at the screen's bottom right

2) Touch it and then you will be allowed to move the modes you want onto the swipe-able bar. After this is done, you will not need to open the More section to find modes to select.

How to Quickly Switch from Rear to Front Camera

1) Open the Camera app and then drag your finger upwards or downwards to easily switch between the back and front camera views.

2) Alternatively, double pressing the power button will also toggle between the front and rear camera views.

CHAPTER FIFTEEN

How to Shoot in HDR10+ Video

The Galaxy S22 can shoot in HDR10+ video. However, this feature is still in its Beta or Labs stage.

1) Launch the Camera app and open Settings.

2) Click on Advanced recording options and you will see the options available for the High Dynamic Range Capture format, however, it is only available when you are shooting 1080p30.

How to Enable Raw Capture

This feature saves pictures like a regular JPEG. To use this feature,

1) Launch the camera app and then click on Settings at the screen's top left corner

2) Proceed to click on Picture Formats.

3) You will see the available options to save Raw copies. Toggle the switch on or off.

4) You can also switch the High Efficiency pictures ((HEIF) on as well.

How to Resize Photos

1) Launch the Gallery App and then choose the picture that you would like to resize.

2) Click on the Edit icon at the screen's bottom.

78

3) Proceed to select the More options which are the three vertical dots at the screen's top right corner.

4) Click on Resize

5) Select your preferred resized image percentage from the resize image options and then click on Done to apply your changes.

6) Click on Save when you have finished editing.

CHAPTER SIXTEEN

How to Enable Voice Commands on Galaxy
S22 Camera App

1) Unlock your phone and click on the Camera apps icon once. Alternatively, you can open the camera from the App drawer.

2) Touch the Gear icon at the top left corner of your screen

3) Navigate through your Camera's settings and click on Shooting methods.

4) Click on the Voice commands toggle in order to activate it. When this is done, you will not be able to start recording videos or click on images using just the S22 voice commands.

1) Launch the camera app from the App drawer on your device and then click on Video.

2) Touch the Auto Framing icon at the bottom corner of your screen to switch the feature on.

3) The icon will give a yellow beam once the feature has been turned on.

   Begin by holding your device a good distance away from the subject to enable them to be seen visibly by the camera. Click on Record to to start filming.

   You will find that once a new subject gets within the viewfinder, the camera will begin following them while still focusing on the original subject.

81

4) When you are done filming, click on Stop to finish.

What are Samsung Galaxy S22 Voice Commands

The voice command feature makes it possible for the device owner to make a video or take pictures using preset commands.

The S22 devices have the following voice commands compatible with them:

- Capture
- Smile
- Cheese
- Shoot
- Record Video

CHAPTER SEVENTEEN

Customizing Camera Settings

Depending on the shooting mode, most options will not be available when you click on the Settings icon from the preview screen.

Intelligent Features

- **Scene optimizer:** This feature sets the Galaxy S22 to control color settings and apply the optimized effect automatically depending on the scene or subject.

- **Shot suggestions:** This feature enables the Galaxy S22 to recommend a composition that would be ideal for your picture.

This is done by recognizing the subject's angle and position.

- **Scan QR codes**: Allow the Galaxy S22 to scan QR codes from the preview screen.

- **Swipe Shutter button to**: Choose a function to be performed when you swipe the camera button to the screen's edge and hold it.

Pictures

- **Picture formats**: Choose the format you would like to save your picture with.

- **High efficiency pictures:** Snap photos with the High Efficiency Image Format (HEIF).

- **RAW copies:** Adjust the Galaxy S22to save photos as uncompressed RAW files (DNG file format) with pro mode. RAW files retain a picture's entire data and gives the best quality. They will, however, consume more space. With the RAW copies feature in use, every picture is saved in two formats — DNG and JPG.

Selfies

• **Save selfies as previewed**: Adjust the Galaxy S22 to download pictures the way they appear on the preview screen when taken with the front camera without flipping them.

• **Selfie color tone:** Choose a tone to apply for taking selfies.

Videos

• **Auto FPS:** Adjust the Galaxy S22 to record brighter videos even with dimly-lit environment by optimizing the frame rate automatically.

• **Video stabilization:** Enable anti-shake in order to eliminate or reduce blurry image as a result of camera shake during video recording.

• **Advanced recording options**: Allow the Galaxy S22 to make use of an advanced recording option.

– **Reduce file size:** It is possible to record videos with the High Efficiency Video Codec (HEVC) format. In order to save space on your phone's memory, the

HEVC videos that have been recorded will be stored as compressed files.

– **HDR10+ videos**: It is possible to record videos each scene optimized in color and contrast.

– **Zoom-in mic**: It is possible to record sound at a higher volume from a zoomed-in direction while you are recording a video.

• It may not be possible to share the HEVC videos online or play them with other devices.

• You will not be able to record slow motion and Super slow-motion videos in the HEVC format.

• The device should support HDR10+ in order to play the HDR10+ video efficiently.

General

• **Auto HDR:** Snap photos using bright and vibrant colors and highlight details even in dark and bright areas.

• **Tracking auto-focus:** Adjust the Galaxy S22 to track and focus on a highlighted subject automatically. Even when the subject is in motion or th camera's position is changed, the camera will still focus on the subject as long as the subject has been selected on the preview screen.

However, there are certain conditions in which tracking a subject may not be successful. These conditions include when the subject is:

> Too small or too big
> Is not steady or is in motion
> Is back-lit or in a dimly-lit environment
> Shares colors or patterns with the background
> Possesses horizontal patterns like blinds.
> Is steady but the camera is shaky.

In situations where the video resolution is high or the optical zoom is used to zoom in or out, the subject tracking may also not be successful.

• **Grid lines:** This feature shows viewfinder guides in an attempt to help composition during subjects' selection.

• **Location tags:** Include a GPS location tag to the picture.

• In locations where the signal is obstructed like in low-lying areas, in-between buildings, or in environments with poor weather conditions, the GPS signal strength may decrease.

• To avoid your location from being visible when you upload your photos on the internet, disable the location tag setting.

• **Shooting methods**: Choose additional shooting methods for recording a video or taking a photo.

• **Settings to keep:** Keep the previously used settings when you open the camera like the shooting mode.

• **Vibration feedback:** Adjust the Galaxy S22 to vibrate in certain conditions like when you click on the camera button.

How to Configure the Shooting Method

1) Click on the Camera icon at the lower right corner of the screen on the Home Screen page.

2) Alternatively, you can swipe upwards or downwards with a finger from the middle of the display and then click on Camera.

   Click on the Settings icon and then select Camera Settings in the upper left part of the screen to open general Camera settings.

Swipe to the right or left in order to navigate through the options that are available from the Camera screen.

Select an option in order to either turn Switch on icon on or off:

- Voice commands
- Floating Shutter button
- Show palm

CHAPTER EIGHTEEN

How to Create/Decorate an AR Emoji Short
Video

You can make a short video using an emoji which can either be used as a call background image or a wallpaper.

1) Open the AR zone app and then click on AR Emoji Studio

2) Click on Create video. Select either Call screen or Lock screen.

3) Choose a template that you prefer. You can click on the gallery icon to modify the background image.

4) Click on Save to store your video file on your device. You can assess the saved videos in the Gallery.

5) Choose an option at the screen's bottom to use the video directly.

This feature makes fun videos or pictures using emojis in different shooting modes.

1) Open the AR zone app and then click on AR Emoji Camera.

2) Choose the emoji and mode that you would like to use. The modes that are available may vary depending on which emoji you choose.

• **SCENE**: The emoji mimics your expressions. You can also change the background image.

• **MASK**: The emoji's face appears over your face so it looks like you are wearing a mask.

• **MIRROR**: The emoji mimics your body movements.

• **PLAY**: The emoji moves on a real background.

3) Click on the emoji icon in order to take a picture or touch and hold your finger over the icon to record a video. It is possible to assess and share the videos and pictures you have captured from the Gallery app.

How To Activate AR Doodle

Create funny videos of people or pets with virtual handwritings or drawings on their faces or anywhere else. When you do this, they do doodle will follow a face that has been recognized as it moves. The doodles that have been created will remain in the same position even when the camera moves.

1) Open the AR Zone and click on AR Doodle. The recognition area will be

visible on the screen once the camera recognizes the subject.

2) Touch the pencil icon to write or draw in the recognition area. You can also draw or write outside the recognition area when you switch to the back camera.

If you click on the rotate icon and then start doodling, you can record yourself as you doodle.

3) Click on the record icon to record a video

4) Touch the Stop icon to end the video recording.

The created video can be viewed or shared from the Gallery. Depending on which camera is in use, the available features on the preview screen may vary.

Albums

Make albums and organize your videos and images.

Open the Gallery app and then click on Albums. Touch the three vertical dots and then select Create album. This will create an album.

Once created, select the album and then proceed to add items by clicking on Add Items. You can then move or copy the videos or pictures you want to the album.

Stories

Anytime that you save or capture videos and images, the Galaxy S22 will read their location tags, date and organize the videos and images and then make stories with them.

Open the Gallery all and then click on stories. Proceed to choose a story.

You can delete or add videos or images by selecting a story and then clicking on the three vertical dots. You can then proceed to tap add or edit.

Syncing Images and Videos

Open the Gallery app and click on the three horizontal lines, then proceed to select settings. Click on Sync with OneDrive and then you follow the instructions that will appear on your screen to finish the sync process. The Cloud and the Gallery app will be synced.

With the Gallery synced with the cloud, videos and pictures taken will also be saved onto the cloud. You can assess the videos and pictures that are saved in the cloud in your Gallery as well as from other devices.

When you connect your Samsung account and Microsoft account, you can set the cloud storage as Microsoft OneDrive.

CHAPTER NINETEEN

Deleting Images or Videos

Open the Gallery app and then click on the three horizontal lines and hold your finger over an image, story or video to delete it and then click on Delete.

Using the Recycle Bin Feature

Deleted videos and pictures can be kept in the recycle bin. These files will be removed once a certain period of time has elapsed.

Open the Gallery app and then click on the three vertical lines. Touch Settings and the click on the Recycle bin switch to turn it on.

You can view files that are in the recycle bin by opening the Gallery, clicking on the three vertical dots and then select the Recycle Bin.

Cropping Enlarged Images

Open the Gallery app and then choose a picture.

Place two finger on the image and spread them apart over the area that you want to save and then tap crop icon.

This will save the cropped portion as a file.

CHAPTER TWENTY

Motions and Gestures

Enable the motion feature and configure settings.

Click on Advanced Features and then select Motions and Gestures.

- **Lift to wake**: Make the Galaxy S22 to automatically turn on the screen when you pick it up.

- **Double tap to turn on screen**: Make the Galaxy S22's screen to turn on when you double-tap anywhere on it while it is turned off.

- **Double tap to turn off screen**: Make the Galaxy S22's screen to go off when you double tap anywhere on it while it is turned on.

- **Keep screen on while viewing:** Make the Galaxy S22's display always on while you are looking at it.

- **Alert when phone picked up**: Make the device notify you once you have new messages or missed calls as soon as you pick up the device.

This feature may not work if the screen is turned on or the device is not on a flat surface.

- **Mute with gestures**: Silence with gestures: Use motions or gestures to mute certain sounds on the device.

- **Palm swipe to capture:** The photographs recorded can be viewed in the Gallery. While utilizing specific programs and functionalities, taking a screenshot is not available. Excessive shaking or an impact to the device may cause an unintended input for some features using sensors.

How to Increase the Timer in Night Mode

The Night Mode analyzes the scene in front of the camera by default and adjusts the shutter speed accordingly.

1) Go to Night Mode and press the Timer icon in the lower-right corner.
2) Choose "Max" and press the Shutter button.

This feature removes undesired reflections and shadows.

1) Use Samsung Gallery to open the image you want to edit.

2) Select the three-dot menu from the drop-down menu.

3) Select Labs. Turn on the Share Eraser and Reflection Eraser toggles now.

4) Return to the previous screen and select Object Eraser.

5) Click the Erase Shadows or Erase Reflections button after drawing around any shadows or reflections you want to remove from the image.

CHAPTER TWENTY- ONE

How To Activate Voice Command

1. To get started, go to the Home screen or the Apps viewer and select Settings.

This brings up the main Settings menu.

2. In the Settings menu, scroll down to Apps and tap it. On the next screen, a list of all installed and downloaded applications will appear.

3. To access the camera app's features and options, look for and tap Camera.

To continue, tap Camera settings.

5. Scroll down the following menu and select Shooting methods.

On the next screen, various shooting methods for the Camera app will be displayed.

6. Toggle the switch next to Voice commands to turn it on.

This activates voice commands for taking pictures and recording movies with the phone's default camera app.

Introduction

Bixby is a user interface that helps you use your device more conveniently.

Samsung's assistant is called Bixby. In 2017, it made its debut on the Samsung Galaxy S8. The virtual assistant can do a lot of things, but it's mostly divided into two parts: Bixby Voice and Bixby Vision.

Starting Bixby

Bixby will launch if you press and hold the side button. To use Bixby, you'll need to be logged into a Samsung account. You can also enable the hot word "Hi Bixby."

Using Bixby

If you use the "Hi Bixby" wake word, you'll be able to converse with your device in natural language, just like you would with Google Assistant. Bixby, on the other hand, appears to be prone to launching by accident, therefore employing the button press approach avoids false identification.

Communications Via Text

You can converse with Bixby via text if your voice is not recognized owing to noise or if you are in a scenario where speaking is difficult.

Start the Bixby app, tap, and then type your request. Bixby will also respond to you via text rather than voice during the conversation feedback.

You can talk to Bixby or type text. Bixby will launch a function you request or show the information you want. Visit www.samsung.com/bixby for more information.

Bixby is only available in some languages, and it may not be available depending on the region.

Bixby Vision

Bixby Vision is a service that makes it easier to learn more about the world around you. Bixby Vision also has accessibility support to help the visually impaired.

Bixby Vision may be found in the More section of the Camera app, on the top left. This will open Vision when you tap it. Bixby Vision has a number of features that utilize the phone's camera. You may either ask Bixby what something is, or open the camera app and press the Bixby Vision button, which works similarly to Google Lens or the Amazon buying app (in the "more" section of the app).

Alternatively, you can launch Bixby Vision using these more ways:

• In the Gallery app, select an image and tap.

• In the Internet app, tap and hold an image and tap Search with Bixby Vision.

• If you added the Bixby Vision app icon to the Apps screen, launch the Bixby Vision app

Using Bixby Vision

1. Open Bixby Vision.

2. Choose a feature which you would like to use.

Using the camera, Bixby Vision can:

1) Recognize QR codes: Using the camera, Bixby Vision is also configured to read barcodes and do shopping by default.

2) Inquire about shopping: Tap the Vision icon in the camera or gallery

app to search, shop, and translate at the touch of a finger.

3) Recognize text from documents or images and extract it.

4) Search for images similar to the recognized object online and related information.

The available features and search results may vary depending on the region or service provider.

How to Use the Quick Share

Content sharing with neighboring devices. Share content with adjacent devices using Wi-Fi Direct or Bluetooth, as well as SmartThings-compatible devices.

1. Open the Gallery app and choose a photo.

2. Open the notification panel on the other smartphone, swipe downwards, and then tap (Quick Share) to activate it. If (Quick Share) isn't visible on the quick panel, press + and drag the button across to add it.

3. Select a device to send the photograph to by tapping Quick Share.

4. On the opposite device, accept the file transfer request.

This functionality does not allow you to share videos with TVs or other SmartThings devices. Use the Smart View feature to watch videos on TV.

With your smartphone, you can control and manage smart appliances and Internet of Things (IoT) gadgets.

To learn more, open the SmartThings app and go to Menu > How to use.

1. Open the SmartThings application.

2. Select Add device or + from the Devices menu.

3. Follow the on-screen steps to select a device and connect to it.

• Depending on the type of connected devices or shared material, several connection techniques may be used.

• Depending on your location, the devices you may connect may differ. The functionality available may vary depending on the linked device.

• The Samsung warranty does not cover the faults or defects of connected devices.

Contact the maker of the connected devices if issues or faults occur.

How to Use the Smart Select

Smart Select is a screenshot-taking function that allows you to take partial or selected screenshots. Simply remove the Samsung's S Pen or press the Stylus Button on the screen to access the shortcut menu. Then go to Smart Select, which lets you drag and draw any shape on the screen to capture it. Rather recording the entire screen and cropping it afterwards in the gallery, it is one of the simplest ways to take a screenshot. Users can also make a GIF that captures the animations in the designated area.

CHAPTER TWENTY -TWO
Accounts and Backup Options

Samsung Cloud allows you to sync, back up, and recover the data on your smartphone. You can also use Smart Switch to login in to accounts like your Samsung or Google account, as well as transfer data to and from other devices.

Tap Accounts and backup on the Settings screen.

• Manage accounts: Sync with your Samsung and Google accounts, as well as other accounts.

• Samsung Cloud: Back up your data and settings and restore the data and settings of your previous device even if you don't have it. For additional information, go to Samsung Cloud.

• Google Drive: Back up your personal data, app data, and device settings to Google Drive. You can make a backup of your important data. To back up data, you must sign in to your Google account.

• Launch Smart Switch to transfer data from your prior device. For further information, see Transferring data from your old device (Smart Switch).

Back up your data on a regular basis to a secure location, such as Samsung Cloud or a computer, so you can recover it if it is corrupted or lost due to an unexpected factory data reset.

Restore your backup data from Samsung Cloud to your device.

1 On the Settings screen, tap Accounts and backup.

2 Tap Restore data and select a device you want.

3 Tick items you want to restore and tap Restore.

How To Reset Camera Settings

The camera application settings on the Samsung Galaxy S22 Camera can be reset to their default levels.

To reset the camera application's settings, follow these steps:

1. Launch the camera app and select >

2. Select Settings.

3. Select General.

4. Choose Yes and Reset.

This choice will only reset the camera application's settings. It will have no effect on the Galaxy Camera's operating system settings, and it will not delete any of your personal data from the camera.

About Director's View Mode on Galaxy S22

Record videos with various angles of view by changing cameras. In this mode, both the subject and the person who is filming can be recorded at the same time.

1 On the shooting modes list, tap **MORE** ➡**DIRECTOR'S VIEW**.

2 Select the screen and the camera thumbnail you want and tap ⦿ to record a video.

- To change the screen before starting the recording, tap and select the screen you want.

- You can change the camera thumbnail while recording. If the thumbnail is hidden, tap ◉ to display it.

3 Tap ☐ to stop recording the video.

Privacy

Privacy Notice: View the privacy notice.

· **Permissions**: View the permissions required to use the Camera app.

- **Reset settings**: Reset the camera settings.

- **About Camera**: View the Camera app version and legal information.

Printed in Great Britain
by Amazon

13406206R00070